EASY EMBROIDERED

MATERIALS

¼" rattail cord
Size 11° seed beads
Size D beading thread in color to
    complement cord

NOTIONS

Size 12° sharps or beading needles
Scissors

Step 1: Measure and cut a length of rattail two times longer than the desired cord length. Fold in half. Using a yard of thread, tie a knot in one end and sew into the cord about 1" from the loop's end. Pass through the center of both cords to connect them.

Step 2: * String enough beads to fit the circumference of both cords. Wrap around the cords and sew through the center of both cords, exiting between beads. Couch (Figure 1) the beads down, exiting at the other side of the cord. Rep from * until the doubled cord is concealed (Figure 2).

Step 3: Proceed couching and wrapping as in Step 2 until you reach 2" from your desired cord length. To create a loop on the other end, fold one side of the cord into a loop and trim the other cord so that you have two cord widths. Secure the ends of the cords and continue wrapping to conceal the join. To finish, tie a knot between beads, sew through the cord, tie off your thread at the cord, and trim thread close to work.

TIPS

- For extra strength, pass back through all the beads for the length of the cord. It also helps to do a little extra couching on every circle of beads.

- Make a continuous bead-embroidered cord, or make breaks between beading to expose the cord (as shown in the example).

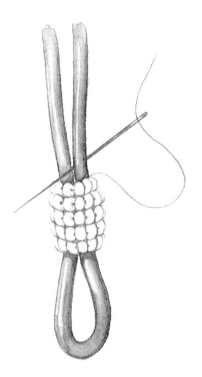

Figure 2

Couching

Also known as "two-thread spot stitch," this technique uses two threaded needles. Begin by passing the needle through the fabric, from wrong side to right side, at the place where the first bead is to go. Thread a number of beads and lay them onto the cloth in your chosen design. With the second threaded needle, come up through the cloth, over the thread between two beads, and back down through the cloth. Repeat this procedure until all the beads lie flat.

Figure 1

DNA SPIRAL CORD

MATERIALS

Size 11° seed beads in two colors
("inside" beads and "outside" beads)
Size D beading thread in color to
complement beads

NOTIONS

Size 12° sharps or beading needle
Scissors

Step 1: String 4 inside beads and 3 outside beads. Tie a knot and pass through the inside beads (Figure 1).

Step 2: String 1 inside and 3 outside beads. Pass through 3 inside beads and pass back through the last inside bead strung (Figure 2). Let these outside beads rest next to previous row's outside beads.

Repeat Step 2 to desired length (Figure 3).

Figure 3

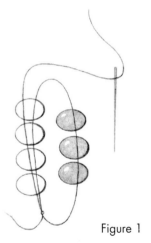

Figure 1

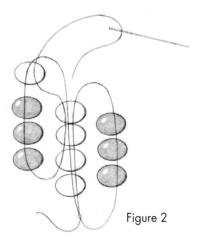

Figure 2

Variations

Experiment with the size of the inside and outside beads.

Increasing and decreasing the numbers of beads on the outside portion will make your cord undulate.

HERRINGBONE CORD

MATERIALS

Any size seed beads
Size D beading thread in a darker color than
  the beads

NOTIONS

Size 12° sharps or beading needle
Scissors

Step 1: Begin with a ladder of six beads (see Rasta Wave, page 27). Join into a foundation circle by passing through the first bead of the ladder. Bring the tail to the top (the opposite side of the beginning tail).

Step 2: Working clockwise, string 2 and pass down through the next bead. This will cause one bead to sit on top of the bead the thread just came out of and one bead to sit on top of the bead you passed down through (Figure 1).

Step 3: Bring the needle up through the next bead (Figure 2).

Steps 4 and 5: Repeat Steps 2 and 3.

Step 6: Repeat Step 2.

Step 7: Pass up through the next bead and the one above it (which is the first bead in the current row, Figure 3).

Repeat Steps 2–7 for each round.

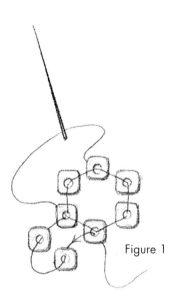

Figure 1

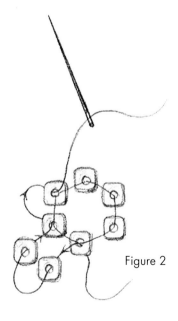

Figure 2

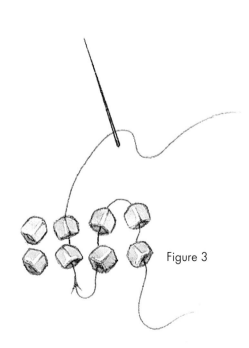

Figure 3

SPOOL-KNITTED CORD

MATERIALS

Size 11° seed beads
Size 8 pearl cotton yarn

NOTIONS

Size 12° beading needle
Wooden spool
Brad nails or staples
Knitting needle or nail
Hammer

Step 1: Hammer four nails or staples into the spool, spacing them evenly around the hole.

Step 2: Thread the needle with yarn, but do not cut the yarn from the ball. String a length of beads that measures one and a half times that of your desired cord length. Slide the beads down and re-wrap the ball.

Step 3: Pass the yarn through the spool and wrap it around your finger to hold taut. The end of the spool without the nails is the end the cord will exit from. Make a loop around each nail with the crossing on the inside of the circle.

Step 4: Slide 1 bead up to the last nail wrapped. *Lay the yarn against the outside of the next nail. Use the knitting needle to pull the first-round loop up and over the nail, securing this second-round yarn. Repeat from * once.

Step 5: Repeat Step 4 twice. Place a single stitch over the bead on the last rnd, then continue with Step 4.

Step 6: Repeat Steps 5 and 6 until you reach the desired length, alternating stitches with and without beads to keep the stitches from bunching up.

Step 7: To finish, bind off the stitches *by taking the first stitch off the nail and placing it on the second nail. Pull the second stitch over the first stitch. Carry the second stitch to the third nail.* Repeat between *s until all the stitches are bound off. Cut the thread and pull the tail through the last stitch.

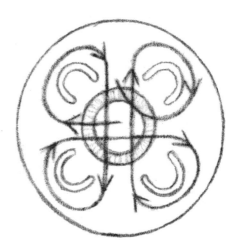

SNAKY PEYOTE CORD

MATERIALS

Size 11° seed beads in four colors
Size D beading thread in color to
    complement beads

NOTIONS

Size 12° sharps needle
Round chopstick
Tape
Scissors

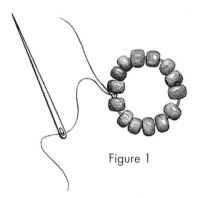

Figure 1

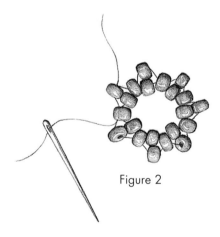

Figure 2

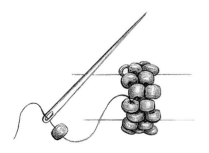

Figure 3

Rnds 1 and 2: String an even number of beads to fit snugly around the chopstick. Leaving a 6" tail, tie the thread in a knot to create a foundation circle (Figure 1). Pass through the first few beads strung to hide the knot and tape the tail to the chopstick.

Rnd 3: *String 1 bead. Skip the next bead on the foundation circle and pass through the next one. Rep from * all around (Figure 2). Pass through the first bead added in this rnd.

Rnds 4 and on: *String 1 bead. Pass through the next bead added in the previous rnd. Rep from * all around. To complete, pass through the first bead added in this rnd.

To finish, use your working thread to tie a knot between beads, and weave through several more beads to secure (Figure 3). Do the same with the tail thread. Trim thread close to work.

Once you have worked two inches of this cord, feel comfortable to remove it from the chopstick. This way you are not bound by the chopstick's length.

BEADED CROCHET CORD

MATERIALS

Seed beads
Fine silk thread or perle cotton

NOTIONS

Crochet hook
Scissors

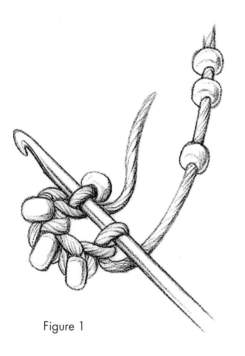

Figure 1

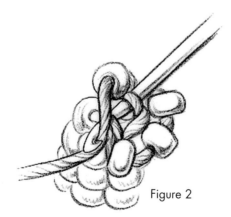

Figure 2

Step 1: Make an initial chain of four (or more) stitches, leaving a bead in each chain stitch by sliding a bead close to the hook before making each stitch.

Step 2: Form a ring of beaded stitches by inserting the hook into the first chain stitch, under the thread carrying the bead (Figure 1). Move the bead to the right side of the hook.

Step 3: Slide a new bead down close to the hook and work a slip stitch by pulling a loop of thread through both loops on the hook. Make a slip stitch with a bead into each of the remaining chain stitches to complete the first round. Continue working beaded slip stitches in a spiral to the length desired (Figure 2).

Spirals and stripes can be made by stringing beads in counted patterns.

CATERPILLAR CORD

MATERIALS

Size 13° seed beads
Size 11° seed beads
Size 6° seed beads
5 mm sequins
Size B beading thread in color to
    complement beads

NOTIONS

Size 12° sharps or beading needle
Scissors

Step 1: String 1 size 6° to use as a tension bead (see page 32). String 3 size 11°s. *String 1 size 6° and 3 size 11°s. Rep from * to reach your desired cord length.

Step 2: Pass back through the last size 6° strung and all the beads strung in Step 1. When you reach the tension bead, remove it and pass through the first four beads strung in Step 1 to create an end loop. Tie a knot between beads.

Step 3: * String 8 size 13°s, 1 sequin, and 1 size 13°. Pass back through the sequin. String 8 size 13°s. Pass through the next size 6° on the inner cord. Rep from * along the cord (Figure 1). When you reach the end, pass through the 3 end beads added in Step 1.

Step 4: Rep Step 2 five times, covering the cord with "spines." *Note:* Steer clear of the previous passes so the spines don't tangle.

> Make this cord as fuzzy as you want by re-peating Step 2. Your only limitation is the amount of thread passes your size 6° beads can handle.

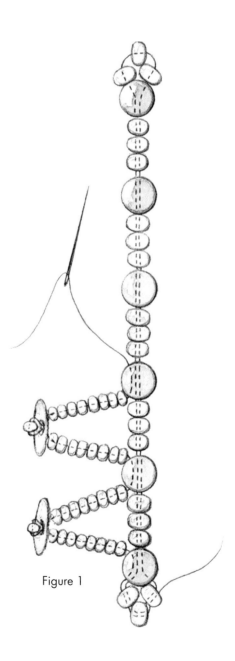

Figure 1

TWISTED CHAIN

MATERIALS

Size 11° seed beads
Size D beading thread in color to
complement beads

NOTIONS

Size 12° beading needle
Scissors
Tape

Step 1: For a 36" long cord, thread about 38" of beads onto each of two 40" lengths of thread.

Step 2: Tie the two threads together at one end with an overhand knot and push the beads toward the knot.

Step 3: Anchor the knotted end on a stable object or hold it in place with your foot. Twist one thread clockwise until it kinks on itself when tension is released.

Step 4: Hold it steady while twisting the other thread clockwise until it kinks on itself. Hold the ends of the two threads together and twist them counterclockwise to wind around each other. Knot the two together on the unknotted end close to the beads.

CADUCEUS CHAIN

Diane Fitzgerald

MATERIALS

15 grams Delicas
10 grams size 14° seed beads
Size D beading thread in color to
    complement beads
Clear nail polish

NOTIONS

Size 12° sharps needles
Beeswax
Scissors

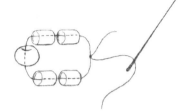

Figure 1

Step 1: Double a 2-yard length of thread. Wax so the strands stick together. String 2 Delicas, 1 seed bead, and 2 Delicas. Tie into a tight foundation circle (Figure 1).

Step 2: String 2 Delicas, 1 seed bead, and 2 Delicas. pass back through the last two Delicas strung in the foundation circle (Figure 2).

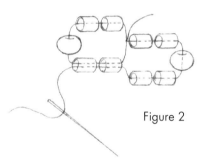

Figure 2

Step 3: *String 1 seed bead and 2 Delicas. Pass back through the last two Delicas added in the prev step (Figure 3). Rep from *, alternating the direction in which beads are added. Keep tension tight. Make a 28"-long chain.

Step 4: *Pass through 12 seed beads on one side of the chain, then pass through 4 Delicas to cross to the other side of the chain. Rep from * back and forth across the chain and pull the thread tight so that the chain curves (Figure 4).

Step 5: Rep Steps 3 and 4 to make another chain.

Step 6: Intertwine the two chains so they cross and wrap around one another but still lie flat. Stitch one chain to the other at the intersections, pass through the beads or around the thread if the bead holes are full.

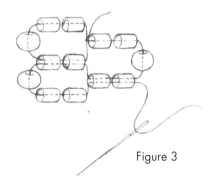

Figure 3

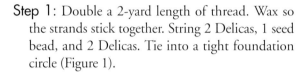

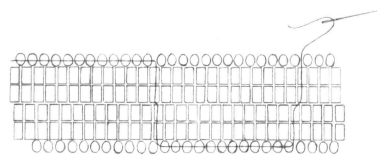

Figure 4

DELICATE WIRE CHAIN

MATERIALS

Size 11° Czech seed beads
6 × 5 oval or other specially shaped beads
Soft Flex® Soft Touch Wire,
Very Fine .010 Diameter

NOTIONS

Wire cutters

Step 1: Measure your desired chain length. Double the length and cut that amount of wire.

Step 2: String 9 seed beads and push them to the center of the wire.

Step 3: String 1 seed bead with one end of the wire and pass back through the same bead with the other end of wire, so the two ends of wire crisscross through the bead.

Step 4: String 2 seed beads, one 6 × 5, and 2 seed beads on each end of the wire.

Step 5: Rep Step 3.

Step 6: String 4 seeds beads on each end of the wire.

Step 7: Rep Steps 3 through 6 until you reach the desired length of chain, ending with Step 3 (Figure 1).

Step 8: Use the wire to tie a knot that can be hidden under the last bead. Weave any excess wire back through the chain.

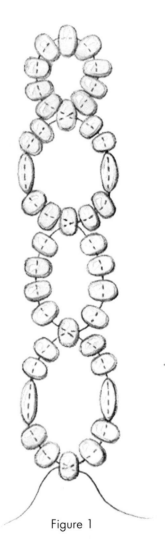

Figure 1

DOUBLE-STRANDED CHAIN

MATERIALS

Size 11° seed beads
Size 6° seed beads
Size D beading thread in color to
    complement beads

NOTIONS

Size 12° beading needle
Scissors

Figure 1

Step 1: Cut a length of thread two and a half times longer than your desired strap length. Use a size 6° to make a tension bead (see page 32) with 6" tail.

Step 2: String 5 size 11°s and pull to the center of the thread. String 1 size 6° and pull it close to the 5 just strung. *String 5 size 11°s and 1 size 6°. Repeat from * to reach your desired strap length.

Step 3: String 5 size 11°s and pass back through the last size 6° strung in Step 2 to create a loop at the end of the strap.

Step 4: *String 5 size 11°s. Pass back through the next size 6° on the strap. Repeat from *, only adding size 11°s, until you reach the other end of the strap (Figure 1). End by passing through the last size 6°.

Step 5: Remove the tension bead. Hold tightly onto the tail thread and pass through the first five 11°s strung in Step 2 to create an end loop. Pass through the next size 6° and tie a knot between threads to secure. Pass through as many other beads as possible to strengthen the strap. Trim your working thread.

Step 6: Weave the tail thread into the beadwork, pass back through the beads from Step 4. Tie a knot between beads to secure and trim close to work.

LINKS

MAXINE PERETZ PRANGE

MATERIALS

9 grams Delicas
Size D beading thread in color to
complement beads

NOTIONS

Size 10° or 12° beading needles
Scissors

Step 1: Make 11 (or any odd number) flat pey-ote strips 3 beads wide by 30 rows long. (See "Maxine's Quick and Easy 3-Bead Flat Pey-ote" at right.) Work the beg tail back into the work. Keep the working-thread tail long enough to later sew each strip into a link.

Step 2: Using the thread you've left at the end of one strip, securely join the ends of one strip to form a circle.

Step 3: Slip the end of another strip through the first link and join the ends to form the next link.

Step 4: Continue adding links until all the strips have been joined.

Step 5: Determine how long you want your fin-ished necklace to be. Take the total desired necklace length (24" slips over most heads without a clasp) and subtract the length of the joined links to determine the length of the strap. Remember that forming the last links when joining the strap to the links will take up some length when linked, so allow extra inches in your calculation—for a 24" finished necklace, I measured the initial 11 links (3") and subtracted that from 24". I added 1¼" (2 × ⅝") for the loss when the ends of the strap became links for a total strap length of 22¼".

Step 6: Slide the end of the strap through the end link and stitch it to itself to form another link. Before sliding the strap through, tem-porarily mark the thirtieth row by sliding a needle through it so that the link it forms is the same as the others. Rep with other side of strap, being careful not to twist the strap.

TIPS

- To keep tension even, pinch the section you've completed between your fingers.
- After adding each bead, secure the work-ing thread over your forefinger and then between your forefinger and middle finger of your anchor hand.

Maxine's Quick & Easy 3-Bead Flat Peyote

Step 1: String 4 beads and slide down the thread, leaving a 6–8" tail (Figure 1).

Step 2: Pass through the second and first beads, forcing the fourth bead to sit on top of the third bead (Figure 2).

Step 2: String 1 bead and Pass through the sec-ond and third beads (Figure 3).

Step 4: Pass through the fourth bead (Figure 4).

Step 5: String 1 bead and pass through the fifth bead (Figure 5).

Step 6: String 1 bead and pass through the sixth and fourth beads (Figure 6).

Step 7: String 1 bead and pass through the sixth and fifth beads (Figure 7).

Step 8: Pass through the seventh bead (Figure 8).

Step 9: String 1 bead and pass through the eighth bead (Figure 9).

Step 10: Rep Steps 6–9, alternating direction depending on thread path, until you reach de-sired length.

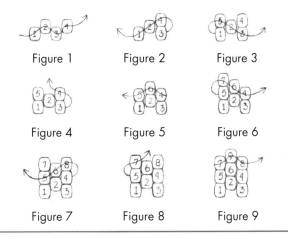

Figure 1	Figure 2	Figure 3
Figure 4	Figure 5	Figure 6
Figure 7	Figure 8	Figure 9

BEADED BRAIDED CHAIN

MATERIALS

Various sizes of seed beads in 5
 coordinating colors
Size D beading thread in color to
 complement beads

NOTIONS

Size 12° sharps or beading needle
Scissors
Tape or pin
Two extra hands

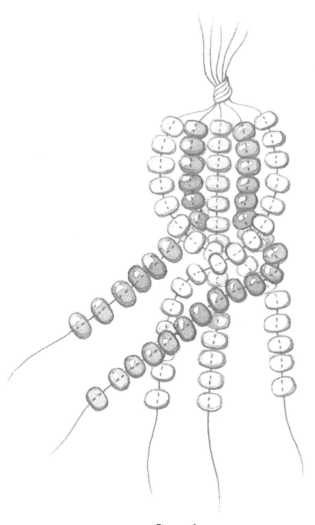

Figure 1

Step 1: Measure 5 lengths of thread at least 16" longer than you want your chain to be and tie them together, leaving a 6" tail at the top. Secure the tied end to a board with tape or a pin.

Step 2: String each strand of thread with one size and color of beads. String a little more for each than you want for the chain. String a tension bead (see page 32) at the end of each strand.

Step 3: Flatten the 5 strands of beads and *separate the far-right and far-left strands. Begin braiding by bringing the far-right strand over the 3 middle strands. Separate the new far-right strand from the others. Cross the far-left strand over the 3 middle strands and separate the new far-left strand from the others. Rep from * until you reach your desired length (Figure 1).

Note: As you braid, you will need to adjust your tension beads when your thread becomes too tight, but be sure not to put too much slack on the strand, or you will have sections of braid that shows thread.

Step 4: Once you have reached your desired length, remove the tension beads and any extra beads on the strands. Use an extra set of hands to tie a knot at the bottom of the chain. One pair of hands needs to hold the top of the braid tightly while the other pair ties the bottom knot.

DAISY CHAIN

MATERIALS

Size 11° seed beads in yellow, gold, and green
Size B dark green beading thread

NOTIONS

Size 12° sharps or beading needle
Scissors

Step 1: String 2 green and 2 yellow and tie a knot to form a circle. Pass through all beads again, exiting from the last yellow strung (Figure 1).

Step 2: String 6 yellow and pass through the yellow beads strung in the previous step. String 1 gold. Pass back through the fourth and third beads just strung (Figure 2).

Step 3: String 2 green and 2 yellow. Pass back through the fourth and third beads strung in the previous step. Pass through the 2 green just strung.

Continue repeating Steps 2 and 3 until you reach your desired chain length.

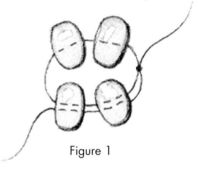

Figure 1

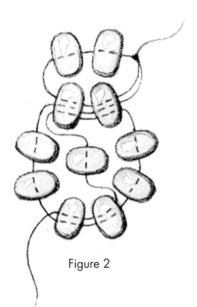

Figure 2

MACRAMÉ STRAP

MATERIALS

Size 6° seed beads
Knotting cord

NOTIONS

Scissors
Tape or pin

Step 1: Cut 8 strands of cord approximately ten times the desired finished length. Tie the ends together and secure the tied end to the work area with tape or a pin.

Step 2: Knot two squares (Figure 1), side by side.

Step 3: String a bead on the two outer cords on one side, then the other. Tie a square with the four center cords.

Step 4: Repeat Steps 2 and 3 to reach your desired strap length.

How to make a square knot

The square knot is made by knotting two cords around two center cords. Make an L shape with the left cord, passing over the two center cords and under the right cord. Pass the right cord under the center cords and through the L. Now make a reverse L with the right cord, passing over the center cords and under the left cord. Pass the left cord under the center cords and through the L.

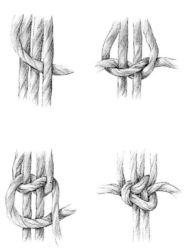

Figure 1

CHIYO'S STRAP

MATERIALS

Size 11° Czech seed beads
Size 8° Czech seed beads
Size D beading thread in color to
complement beads

NOTIONS

5 size 10° or 12° beading needles
Scissors
Tape or pin

Step 1: Cut five lengths of thread 12" longer than your desired strap length. Tie all at the top, leaving a 6" tail. Tape or pin the tied end to a board or table.

Step 2: String 16 size 11° beads on each thread.

Step 3: String 8 size 8° beads on one thread and snug to the beads strung in Step 2. Pass each other thread through these 8 beads to create one strand (Figure 1).

Step 4: Rep Steps 2 and 3 until the strap reaches the desired length. Tie off at the end.

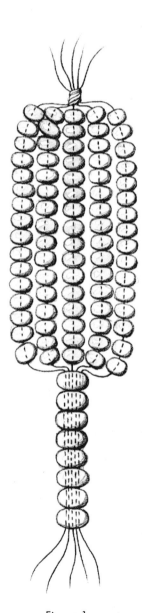

Figure 1

LOOMWORKED STRAP

MATERIALS

Size 11° Czech seed beads
Size D beading thread in color to
  complement beads

NOTIONS

Bead loom
Size 12° beading needle
Scissors

Step 1: Warp your loom according to manufacturer's directions to accommodate the strap's bead width.

Step 2: Use a yard of thread and secure it to the first warp thread by tying a knot.

Step 3: String the number of beads needed for the first row onto the weft thread and slide them down to the knot. Bring the beaded weft thread *under* the warp threads and push the beads up with your finger so there is one bead between each two warp threads.

Step 4: Hold the beads in place and pass back through all the beads, making sure that this time the weft thread passes *over* the warp threads (Figure 1).

Step 5: Rep Steps 2–4 for each row of beads until you reach your desired strap length.

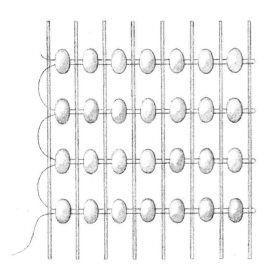

Figure 1

RIGHT-ANGLE WOVEN STRAP

MATERIALS

Any size seed beads
Size B beading thread in color to
complement beads

NOTIONS

Size 12° sharps or beading needle
Scissors

Figure 1 refers to bead positions—
these are not bead numbers, but position numbers.

Row 1: String four base beads. Pass
through the beads in positions 1, 2,
and 3. The bead in position 3 will
become the bead in position 1 in
the next group. String three beads.
Pass through the bead in position 3
of the last group (now position 1 of
this group), and the bead in position 2 and the bead in position 3
(now position 1 of the next group).
String 3.

Continue working in this pattern until
the row comes to your desired
width. In the last group, pass
through the beads in positions 1, 2,
3, and 4.

Row 2: String 3. Pass through the bead
in position 4 of the previous group
and the bead in position 1 of this
group. String 2. Pass through the
bead in position 2 of Row 1, the
bead in position 1 of the previous
group, and the beads just added.
Pass through the bead in position 4
of Row 1. String 2. Pass through
the bead in position 2 of the previous group and the bead in position
4 of Row 1. Pass through the first
bead just added. String 2. Pass
through the bead in position 2 of
Row 1, the bead in position 1 of
the previous group, and the first
bead just added.

Row 3: Repeat Row 2.

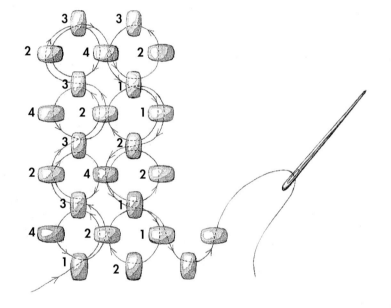

ALPHABET SOUP STRAP

MATERIALS

Size 11° seed beads in colors A and B
Size B beading thread in color to complement beads

NOTIONS

Size 12° sharps or beading needle
Scissors

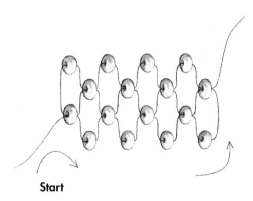

Start

Rows 1 and 2: Using a yard of thread and leaving a 6" tail, string 6 A.

Row 3: String 1 A. Pass back through the fifth bead strung in the previous step. String 1 A. Pass back through the third bead strung in the previous step. String 1 A. Pass back through the first bead strung in the previous step. Tie a knot using the tail and working threads.

Rows 4 and on: String 1 A. Pass through the last bead strung in Row 3. Continue across, adding beads in the "empty" spaces. Once you've established a rhythm, begin using the alphabet chart below.

> Beading an alphabet evokes an old-time sampler. Also consider beading a message, lyrics to a song, or a stanza from your favorite poem to enhance the piece to which your strap is attached.

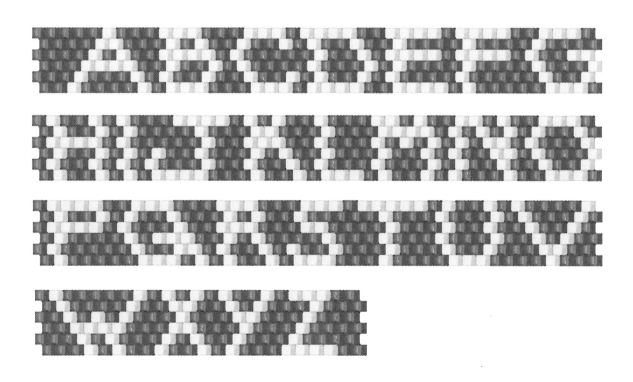

SUPER STRONG SQUARE-STITCHED STRAP

MATERIALS

Size 11° Czech or Japanese seed beads
Size 6° seed beads
Size D beading thread in color to
complement beads

NOTIONS

Size 12° sharps needle
Scissors

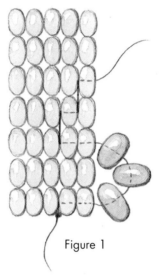

Figure 1

How to Do Square Stitch

Begin by stringing a row of beads. For the second row, string two beads, pass through the second-to-the-last bead of the first row, and passing back through the second bead of those just strung. Continue by stringing one bead, passing through the third-to-last bead of the first row, and passing back through the bead just strung. Repeat this looping technique across to the end of the row.

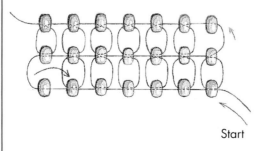

Start

Step 1: Use size 11° beads to square stitch a 12-bead-wide strap to the desired length.

Step 2: Using a new length of thread, tie an anchor knot between the beads at one end of the strap. Weave your thread to exit the corner bead.

Step 3: String 3 size 6° seed beads and pass through the end bead of the strap's third row.

Step 4: Weave the thread through two rows of beads and pass back through the end bead of the strap's fifth row.

Step 5: Repeat Steps 3 and 4, passing through and passing back through the end bead of every other row, until the entire side is covered with the picot fringe.

Step 6: Repeat Steps 2 through 5 on the other side of the strap.

BUBBLE FRINGE

MATERIALS

Size 11° seed beads or Delicas
Size D beading thread in color to
    complement beads

NOTIONS

Size 12° sharps or beading needle
Scissors

Figure 1

Step 1: Anchor the thread in your fabric or beadwork base. String 70 beads.

Step 2: Skipping 7 beads from the last bead strung, pass back through the eighth through thirteenth beads. This will form a loop, or "bubble," at the bottom of the fringe with beads 1 through 6.

Step 3: Count up to the twentieth bead and pass back through beads 21 through 28, forming the second bubble with beads 14 through 19.

Step 4: Count up to the thirty-ninth bead and pass back through beads 40 through 44, forming the larger third bubble with beads 29 through 39.

Step 5: Count up to the fifty-ninth bead and pass back through beads 60 through 70 (Figure 1), forming the last and largest bubble to finish one fringe leg.

DAISY FRINGE

MATERIALS

Size 11° seed beads in three colors
(A, B, and C)
Size D beading thread in color to
complement beads

NOTIONS

Size 12° sharps or beading needle
Scissors

Step 1: Anchor the thread in your fabric or bead-work base. String 7 A and 6 B.

Step 2: Pass through the first four B strung in Step 1 (Figure 1).

Step 3: String 1 C. Pass back through the first B and all the A beads strung in Step 1.

Step 4: Repeat Steps 1–3 for each fringe leg.

VARIATIONS

- Try using different sized beads for the petals and flower center.

- Make a larger daisy by increasing the number of B beads.

- Vary the A beads along your fringe line to get a garden effect.

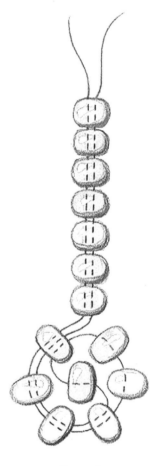

Figure 1

LEAF FRINGE

BARBARA L. GRAINGER

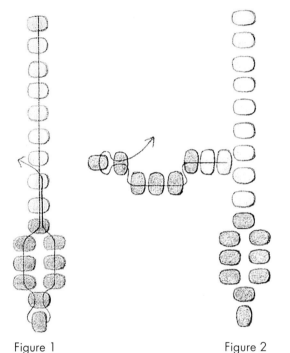

Figure 1   Figure 2

Step 1: String a tension bead leaving a 6" tail. String the desired length of vine-colored beads and 6 leaf beads. Pass back through the second bead from the end.

Step 2: String 3 leaf beads. Pass back through the first leaf bead and two of the vine beads (Figure 1).

Step 3: String 2 vine beads and 6 leaf beads. Pass back through the second bead from the end (Figure 2).

Step 4: String 3 leaf beads. Pass back through the first leaf bead, 2 vine beads, and 2 branch beads, working up the branch toward the top of the fringe (Figure 3).

Rep Steps 3 and 4 until the vine is full of leaves.

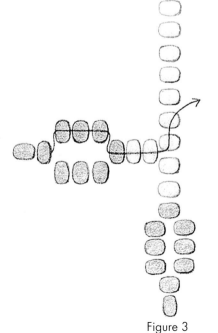

Figure 3

DESIGN TIP

As you cover your fabric base or piece of bead-work with this fringe, vary the amount of A beads you string in Step 1 to create what looks like a jungle of leaves. Dot your jungle with Daisy Fringe (page 22) to complete the look.

TWISTED FRINGE

MATERIALS

Size 11° seed beads
Accent beads
Size D beading thread in color to
complement beads

NOTIONS

Size 12° beading needle
Scissors

Step 1: Anchor the thread in your fabric or bead-work base. String enough seed beads to reach the desired fringe length. String 1 (or more) accent beads; these beads will be the end of the fringe. String a length of seed beads equal to the length of those just strung.

Step 2: Slide your needle close to the last bead and twist the needle between your thumb and forefinger (Figure 1).

Step 3: While holding the accent bead, secure the thread to the base. The beads will twist up on themselves (Figure 2).

TIPS

- Make the same number of twists (Step 2) for each fringe leg so all legs are even.

- Dangle beads can be added by passing back through a group of accent beads (Figure 3). Be sure to match the twists in the upper part of the fringe above the accent beads.

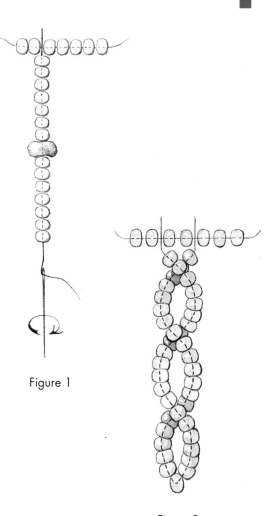

Figure 1

Figure 2

VICTORIAN CHAIN EDGING

MATERIALS

Size 11° seed beads (purple)
Size 10° seed beads (green)
7 × 5 teardrop cut-glass beads
Size B beading thread in color to
    complement beads

NOTIONS

Size 12° sharps or beading needle.
Scissors

> This sturdy edging—a flat beaded chain with added fringe—is made separately and then sewn to the base.

NETTED CHAIN

Step 1: Leaving a 10" tail, string 5 purple beads and 1 green bead. Pass back through the last purple strung so that the green bead forms a pointed cap on the string of beads. String 3 purple and pass back through the first bead strung (Figure 1).

Step 2: String 2 purple and 1 green. Pass back through the second of the last group of 3 purple strung (the third purple from the previous green cap). Repeat Step 2 to desired length. Weave the thread through the beads so that it exits from the last green bead added.

FRINGE

Step 3: String 3 green, 1 drop, 1 green. Pass back through the drop and 1 green. String 2 green. Pass through the next green point and weave the thread through the net to exit from second green point. Repeat Step 3.

Step 4: Attach the netting to the base through the top green point beads. Weave the thread tails into the netting, tying knots after a few crosses. Trim close to work.

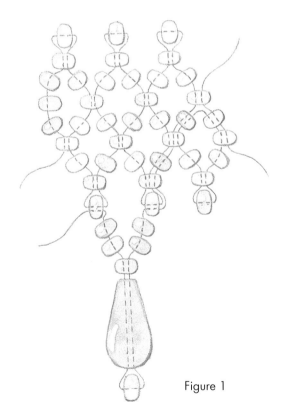

Figure 1

KINKY FRINGE

MATERIALS

Size 11° seed beads
Size D beading thread in color to
complement beads

NOTIONS

Size 12° sharps or beading needle
Scissors

Step 1: Anchor the thread in your fabric or beadwork base. String 15 to 20 beads. This is your base row. Skip the last bead and pass back through 6 to 8 beads. Pull the thread taut.

Step 2: String 6 to 8 beads. Skip the last bead and pass back through the beads just strung.

Step 3: Pass back through 6 to 8 beads of the base row, moving toward the top (Figure 1).

Step 4: Repeat Steps 2 and 3 until you reach the end of the base row.

TIPS

• Work the legs of this fringe very close to one another to create the appearance of a coral bed.

• Use a brightly contrasting bead at the end of each "kink" for a striking look.

Figure 1

MATERIALS

Size 11° seed beads
Size D beading thread in color to
    complement the beads

NOTIONS

Size 12° sharps or beading needle
Scissors

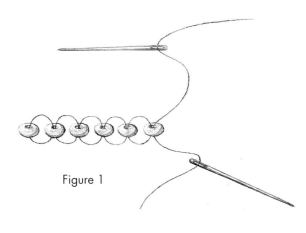

Figure 1

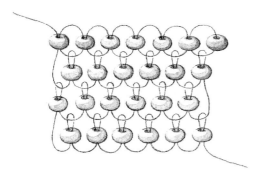

Figure 2

Figure 3

Row 1: Create a row of ladder stitch (Figure 1) that reaches the length of your fabric or beadwork base. Sew the ladder along the edge of your base.

Row 2: *String 1 bead. Pass through the closest exposed thread loop on the ladder created in Row 1. Pass back through the bead just strung. Rep from * across the row (Figure 2).

Row 3: String 2 beads. Pass through the closest exposed thread loop of the previous row. Pass through the second bead just strung. *String 1 bead. Pass through the closest exposed thread loop of the previous row. Rep from * across the row.

Row 4: String 2 beads. Pass through the closest exposed thread loop of the previous row. Pass through the second bead just strung. Continue across in regular brick stitch (as you did in Row 3). When you've added 10 beads, do an increase by working 2 beads at one thread loop (Figure 3).

Row 5: Work this row in regular brick stitch, taking care to work the beads added in the previous row.

Row 6: Create the row in regular brick stitch with an increase (like Row 4) after every 12 beads. Be sure that your increase lies below the increase points created in Row 4.

Row 7: Rep Row 5. Note that your edging will start to warp and twist. This begins the ruffle effect.

Row 8: Create the row in regular brick stitch with an increase (like Row 4) after every 14 beads. Again, be sure that your increase lies below the increase points created in Row 4 and 6.

Rows 9 and 10: Rep Row 5.

LOOPED FRINGE

MATERIALS

Assorted beads
Size B beading thread in color to
complement beads

NOTIONS

Size 12° sharps or beading needle
Scissors

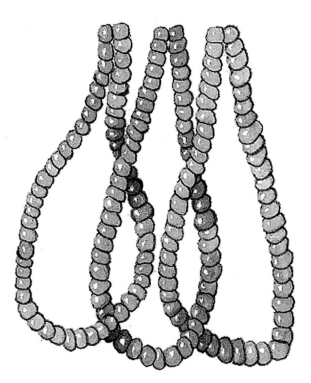

Figure 1

Step 1: Anchor the thread in your fabric or bead-work base. String enough beads to form a loop. *Pass through the base near the top of the loop and exit ¼" along the base.

Step 2: String the same amount of beads as in Step 1. Pass through the loop back to front (or front to back; just be consistent). Repeat from * to make a row of loops (Figure 1).

TIPS

- Mix bugle and crystal beads in a symmetrical fashion for a Victorian look.

- Scatter semi-precious stones about the loops for an organic feel.

- Make long loops and pass back through each loop more than once to create twisted loops.

ART DECO FRINGE

MATERIALS

Size 11° seed beads
6mm flat round disk beads (holes drilled
   lengthwise)
Specialty drop bead (this sample employs
   paw-shaped beads)
Size B beading thread in color to
   complement beads

NOTIONS

Size 12° sharps or beading needle
Scissors

Step 1: Make a 1" strip of flat peyote three
   beads wide (see "Links," page 12). End
   the strip with a single center bead. Tie a
   knot between beads and pass back
   through the last bead added on the strip.

Step 2: String 1 round disk, 3 seed beads, 1
   drop, 3 seed beads, and pass back through
   the round disk (Figure 1). Pass through
   the last bead added on the peyote strip
   and all the beads added in this step. Tie a
   knot at the thread between beads. Weave
   through several beads on the peyote strip,
   tie another knot if desired, and trim
   thread close to the work.

Step 3: Create several fringe legs and sew
   them at ¼" distances either into existing
   beadwork or into fabric.

Figure 1

STRAIGHT LEG FRINGE

MATERIALS

Size 11° seed beads
Small drop beads or magatamas
Size B beading thread

NOTIONS

Size 12° sharps or beading needle
Scissors

Step 1: String as many beads as you want for the finished length of the fringe plus 1 accent bead.

Step 2: pass back through all the beads before the last accent bead.

Step 2: Pass through edging and rep from Step 1.

The most basic of fringes, this one is versatile and goes with just about anything. Put it on a lampshade, on a T-shirt, on the headliner around a windshield, or even around your hat brim to keep pesky slow-moving flies away.

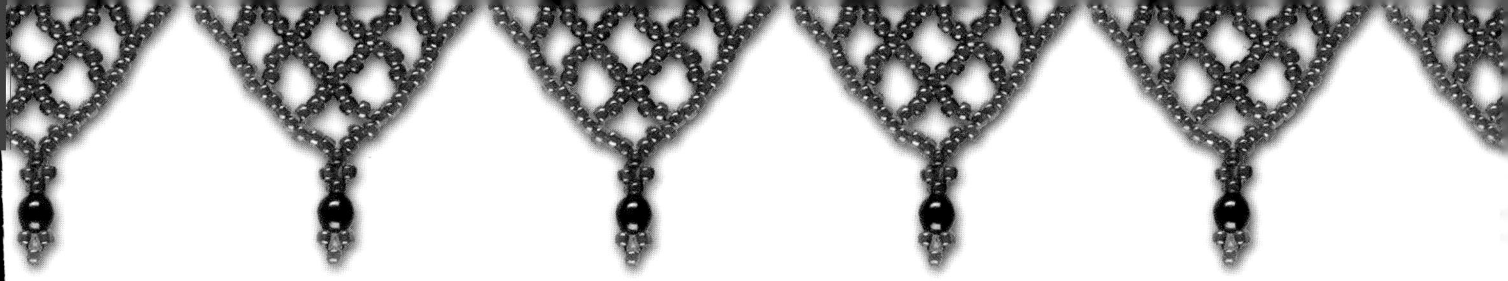

NETTED TRIANGLES

MATERIALS

Size 11° Czech seed beads
6 × 5 drop bead
Size D beading thread in color to
complement beads

NOTIONS

Size 12° sharps or beading needle
Scissors

Row 1: If you are attaching this fringe to fabric, begin by sewing 20 seed beads to the edge so that they lie hole-to-hole. This is your foundation row. (If you are attaching the fringe to beadwork, secure your thread and weave through the first 20 beads from the edge.) Exit from the twentieth bead.

Row 2: String 7 seed beads. Skip 4 foundation row beads from the end and pass back through the fifth foundation row bead. *String 7 seed beads. Skip another 4 foundation row beads and pass back through the fifth foundation row bead. Repeat from * twice. This creates your first row of "nets."

Row 3: Pass back through the fabric base (or the beadwork) and the last 4 beads strung in the previous row. Turn your work over. String 7 seed beads. Pass back through the fourth bead of the second net in the previous row. Continue across, creating two more nets. Weave your thread through the beads so you pass back through the last 4 beads added in this row.

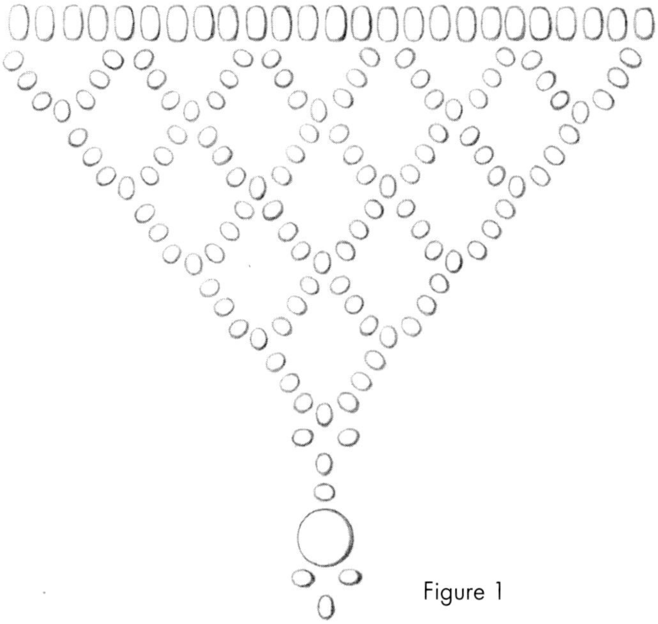

Row 4: Rep Row 3, creating only 2 nets for this row.

Row 5: String 6 seed beads and 1 drop. Pass back through the sixth seed bead. String 1 seed bead. Pass back through the fourth bead originally strung in this row. String 3 seed beads. Pass back through the fourth bead of the first net created in Row 4. Weave your thread through several beads and tie a knot to secure. Trim working thread close to work.

Figure 1

Create a series of these netted triangles to embellish a scarf, pillow, or piece of beadwork.

FINDINGS

Use these items to finish off your cords, chains, and straps to make bracelets and necklaces.

Lobster clasps   Spring rings   Sister clasps

Lobster clasps, spring rings, and sister clasps can be attached to thread with knots or crimp beads. The clasps lock onto a jump ring attached at the other end of the thread.

Multi-strand clasps have several holes for attaching threads from a piece with multiple strands. Secure thread with knots or crimp beads.

Barrel clasps

Barrel and torpedo clasps are very secure—one side screws into the other for locking. The larger style is usually called "barrel" and the smaller, oval style is called "torpedo." Attach them to cords with knots or crimp beads.

Torpedo clasps

Hook and eye clasps are just that—attach the hook to one end of a piece and the eye to the other end. Because the clasp works with gravity, it is good to use with pieces that have some weight (on lighter pieces, the hook and eye tend to travel apart).

End cones cover the ends of beadworked chains, thin loomwork, or thick thread. They act as a transition between the chain body and finding assembly. String thread through end tip and connect finding assembly with knots or crimp beads.

End caps are metal half-spheres used to cover the end of beadworked chains. They act as a transition between chain body and finding assembly. String thread through the end cap hole and connect the finding assembly with knots or crimp beads.

Tension Bead A tension bead (or stopper bead) holds your work in place. To make one, string a bead larger than those your are working with, then pass through the bead again, making sure not to split your thread. The bead will be able to slide along, but will still provide tension to work against when you're beading the first two rows.

Tying and adding new thread Once your thread has 4" left, use the thread that lies between beads to anchor your working thread. Do so by tying an overhand knot with your working thread to the thread between beads. Pass through several more beads and tie another knot between beads. Pass through a few more beads to hide the last knot. Remove your needle and trim the thread close to the work.

Start a new thread in a similar way by tying knots between beads, always hiding the knot by Pass through a few more beads and pulling tight.

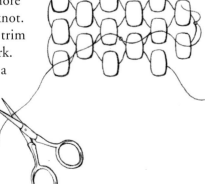